Self-Defense: The Complete Self-Defense Guide against Unexpected Fights and Sudden Attacks

Danger is always amongst us. Whether it is unexpected assailants, street fights or armed criminals, at any time, the worst could happen, and if you have no means of defending yourself, your well-being can be easily be threatened. You have to find an effective way to protect yourself from harm. Proper self-defense discipline can be the countermeasure that protects a person's health and well-being. Broadly speaking, there are three aspects to this discipline: physical, mental, and behavioral. Ideally, you have to train yourself and master all the defense strategies so that you can protect yourself, however necessary. Dangers come in various forms, and your defensive countermeasure should effectively meet harm according to its demand.

This book is designed as a guide to help beginners enter the world of self-defense. It is the aim of the book to improve your stance and confidence against danger so that you can effectively fend for yourself, as well as others.

There is a strong need for self-protection because, in the face of danger, your best chance of survival begins and ends with your personal effort. In the heat of danger, you need to know how to deal with it, so that you can protect yourself. In order to properly defend yourself against most common unexpected attacks, it is not necessary to become an expert in this field, but some knowledge and practice can really go a long way. It all starts somewhere.

"I don't even call it violence when it's in self-defense; I call it intelligence."

-Malcolm X-

Table of Contents

Chapter 1 - Physical Defense 5
    Unarmed and Armed Defense 6
    Defensive Techniques 12

Chapter 2 - Useful Defensive Tips and Tricks 18
    Self Defense Drills 24

Chapter 3 - Mental Defense 40
    Developing the Correct Mindset 40

Chapter 4 - The Scope and Limitations of Physical and Mental Self-Defense 50
    Other Forms of Self Defense 54

Conclusion 65

Chapter 1 - Physical Defense

The most common form of self-defense involves physical force or action. This may be performed armed or unarmed, depending on mastery of skill, and its success is dependent on various parameters. So if you are after achieving the highest success rate, the most effective defensive approach is one that measures the personal capability of the individual.

Ultimately, your training should determine your level. It is not the mere punch that makes a person bleed, but the skill with which the punch is thrown. It is more than the mere ownership of a gun, but the precision of your aim. There is so much more to self-defense that meets the eye. It is not the violence and physicality of the act, but the technicality of your attempt to defend yourself.

You may be a woman and small in build, but that does not mean that you cannot defend yourself physically. This book will make you understand your capacity to make a difference in times of threat.

Unarmed and Armed Defense

Physical defense is two-fold: unarmed and armed. Unarmed physical defense can go from basic to advanced, depending on the training. It could be as simple as learning how to escape from dangerous knife and gun situations to actually carrying out a combination of martial arts styles and techniques to forward an attack. Armed physical defense utilizes weapons, depending on skill and availability. The most common weapons are your everyday materials, such as pens, keys, kitchen utensils and so forth. They may be more injurious, as in the case of knives, tasers, pepper sprays and guns.

There are many self-defense disciplines and martial arts that you can apply to your own learning, but not all of them transfer properly to real life situations. The following are some of the disciplines you can consider taking for this purpose:

- Krav-Maga: Hand-to-hand combat system that is a no-nonsense and practical approach to self-defense. There are no weapons, no special tools, which is why it is so easy to apply to real life.

- Defendo: Started in 1945, Bill Underwood (Canada's top unarmed instructor in World War II) developed this martial art for application in various law enforcement agencies. It has jujitsu roots and is an unarmed combat, modified specifically for self-defense.

- Systema: A Russian martial art discipline which is a hybrid of armed and unarmed fighting. It involves grappling, hand-to-hand combat, firearms training, and knife fighting. It is a martial art that focuses on the delivery of fluid movements, designed to destroy the momentum of an attacker.

- Jujitsu: This is a Japanese martial art designed to defend against unarmed or armed attack. Its principles revolve around using the attacker's strength against him and involve neutralizing moves achieved through throws, pins and joint locks.

- Rape Aggression Defense (RAD). Is a self-defense program that involves four principles: education, self-dependency, making decisions and the realization of one's power. It is a program for women so they may learn about defense and resistance.

- Reality Based Self Defense (RBSD). As the name suggests, it focuses on reality-based circumstances that are independent of any known art of fighting. It trains the student to carry out throws, elbows, and various standing submissions that may be applied to real world self-defense scenarios. It touches on the physical, psychological, emotional, tactical, legal and moral perspective of fighting.

- Kickboxing: It is a stand-up sport based kicking and punching with roots from Muay Thai, karate, western boxing and Khmer boxing. It is utilized as a contact sport and general fitness workout; with applications in self-defense.

- Boxing: This is a viable form of self-defense since unarmed attackers will usually be using their fists. This classic discipline teaches you how effectively meet, deflect and defend yourself against punches.

- Muay Thai: With origins from Thailand, this stand-up combat sport is a physical and mental discipline that utilizes the "art of eight limbs." Its interesting name basically signifies the perfect use of both pairs of elbows, fists, shins, and knees.

- Savate: Also known as French boxing, "savate," is a French word that means old shoe and it is a creative combat sport that makes use of feet and hands as weapons.

- Shoot Boxing: This is a stand-up fighting combat sport with roots from Japan and makes use of punches, kicks, throws, knees, throws, elbows and various standing submissions.

- MMA: Also known as Mixed Martial Arts, is a full-contact combat sport that involves moves such as grappling and striking. Opponents are allowed to stand up or stay on the ground.

- Sambo: SAMBO is a Soviet combat sport and martial art used by the Soviet Red Army and stands for Samozashchita Bez Oruzhiya, which translates as "self-defense without weapons." It was first introduced in 1920 and involves hand-to-hand combat. There are three types of Sambo: combat, sport, and freestyle.

- Wrestling: The most significant move in wrestling is grappling. The goal is to throw an opponent or to hold them down. Much of this is performed on the floor. Although there is arguably limited application in real-life for this discipline, it can be a useful skill to know how to react when you're on the ground. It can be a good complement to other forms of self-defense.

- BJJ: Also known as Brazilian jiu-jitsu and it is a martial art and combat sport that involves grappling and fighting on the ground, like wrestling.

- Sanshou: This is a martial art discipline that was developed by the Chinese military. It has roots from Kung fu, but it has been modified to include more modern combat techniques.

- Karate: This is an unarmed combat that involves moves performed by both hands and feet. It became popular in Japan in 1920, but it has Chinese origins, in the Tang dynasty. The word "karate" means empty hands, signifying the fact that it is a discipline involving no weapons.

- Kung Fu: Also known as "wushu" this is so much like karate, and it is a Chinese martial art. It is a study, and so much more than a martial art, that develops not just the skill but the discipline of combat.

- Taekwondo: This has Korean origins, and it means "the way of the food and the fist." It involves a lot of high kicks, spinning and jumping kicks, head-height kicks, and fast kicking kicks.

- Pencak: This has Indonesian roots, it is also known as Pencak silat, and it is a full-body combat discipline that involves grappling, striking and throwing.

- Hapkido: This is another Korean martial art which involves kicking and various circular movements. It is a discipline that is concentrated on the use of coordinated strength. It is a useful self-defense technique that involves a lot of grappling, joint locking, and throwing. But it also makes use of weapons and traditional fighting moves. In this case, it may be applied for both close-range and long-range situations.

- Silat: This is a Malay martial art discipline that is very good for self-defense. It is an indigenous martial art that has applications that are seen in various Asian fighting traditions.

- Eskrima: This is a Filipino martial art discipline and is also known as Arnis or Kali. In the Philippines, this is a national sport but is has great applications for various self-defense situations. Eskrima is an armed combat that makes use of sticks, bladed weapons, knives, and various improvised weapons. It also involves various hand-to-hand combat as well as grappling and joint locking.

The effectiveness of your unarmed or armed attack will rely on your capability to aim. Your knowledge of your enemy's vulnerability is a strength and advantage you ca rely on. There are six main damage areas that you have to concentrate on, if you want to bring injury in the most effective manner: the groin, knee, leg, neck, neck, ears and nose.

Defensive Techniques

When you find yourself in the middle of a situation, you have to assess the danger, and when contact is necessary and unavoidable, you need can carry out the following techniques:

1. Get Loud and Push Back

    As soon as your attacker comes near, should shout "back off" as loudly as you can and push him away. Your goal is to get help from anyone nearby. You get loud and push back, first and foremost, so that any potential rescuers can come to your defense. In some cases, the attacker is alarmed by this move and flees. You are lucky if he does. If he continues to attack, you move on to your next level of defense.

2. Hitting the Eyes

    You can launch an effective escape by interfering with the vision of your attacker. Gough, scratch or poke the eyes with your fingers or knuckles. Aim straight for the sockets.

3. Striking the Nose

    Using the heel of your palm, throw the weight of your entire body and strike a force up your attacker's nose, straight to the nasal bones. If your attacker is at your back, you may hit the front or side of his nose, using your elbow. Hitting the nose will inflict so much pain; it will disarm your attacker for a considerable time.

4. Chopping the Neck

With perfect aim, you can bring great damage to the jugular vein or the carotid artery, when you chop the neck. Using a knife hand strike, keep your fingers straight and bound tightly, and chop the neck area with some serious force. If your attacker is positioned conveniently, use the tip of your elbow and thrust upward or downward, straight to your attacker's throat, pushing all your weight forward.

5. Slicing the Knee

Kick the side of your attacker's knee and cause temporary injury on your attacker. Aiming for the side will immediately cause an imbalance that you can cause great advantage of. Kicking the front of the knee will be more injurious, but success is lower. The side of the knee is more vulnerable, so just make sure that you can carry out the slicing movement without getting your foot grabbed.

6. Freedom from the Wrist Hold

If your hands or wrists have been captured by your attacker, the usual reaction is to pull back to be able to get away from the hold. That technique is never going to be effective. So, while you are being held at the wrist, stabilize yourself with a squat and instead of moving away from him, bend your elbow and let it touch his forearm until you come to an angle his hands can no longer take. At some point, your hard will break free from his hold.

7. Don't Be Pinned Down

If your attacker has pinned you down on the floor, your goal is to flip things and get on top. If the attacker is on top of you and his hands are on your neck, use your right hand to hold his right wrist, your left hand to hold his right elbow and your left leg to trap is right leg. While this is secure, lift your pelvis to destabilize him and flip positions.

8. Freedom from the Bear Hug

The easiest way to break free from the bear hug is to stomp at your attacker's feet. If this does not work, drop your weight as if you are doing a squat and try to hit the head of your attacker using your elbows.

9. Kicking the Groin

The groin is one of the most vulnerable areas. To do this, you have to gain a stable stance first. Using your stable leg, behind you, raise your leg straight and upward, leaning your back for balance.

10. Counterattacking the Outside Strike

If you are about to receive a blow coming from the outside or the sides, you have to stretch your arms and fingers out, and with your elbows bent a little, raise your arms to stop the oncoming blow from your attacker. Then use your other arm to plant a punch on your attacker's face.

11. Escaping the Two-Handed Choke

First of all, determine which leg is staggering behind you. If this is the left, raise your left arm straight. Cross the left leg behind the right and turn back, to the direction of the raised arm. This should put pressure on your attacker's wrists so you can break free.

12. Heel Down the Shin

If someone comes from behind you, the best way to conquer your attacker is to run your heel down the front of his shin or the bone in front of their lower leg. He will, most likely, not see it coming. You just have to lift your heel, and if you are wearing the right type of shoes, you can do damage with just one swift move.

13. Hitting the Nose with the Head

Another way to deal with an attacker who chooses to grab you from behind is to aim for the nose. To work on a perfect head butt, all you have to do is to throw your head back with all your strength and do so by aiming for your attacker's nose. The nose is very sensitive, and if you succeed in inflicting enough pain, you will be released by your attacker.

14. The Ear and Eye Grab

If your at your from, from the front, you can grab his ear and use your firm grip on either side, to pivot to the eye sockets. Grabbing on the ear will allow you to automatically hit the eye so you can put all the weight on the socket to poke the eyes and cause him to jerk back. If you do this right, you will gain leverage to escape from your attacker.

15. Crushing the Windpipe

The windpipe is the passageway of air down the throat. It is also the source of the sound and is found just below the Adam's apple. Using two fingers, poke into the space between the Adam's apple and the breastbone. If you feel it, there is a hollow space that actually dips around the neck area. To incur damage on your attacker, you need to press hard on that area to keep him from breathing. This will make your attacker grasp his throat and release you, in the process.

16. The Key As Your Weapon

Walking to the car, at night, is often quite ominous. You can start a good habit of walking with your key clasp in your first, and the tip poking in between the fingers. If in case you get attacked, you can use the key in your hand to slash your attacker's face and put him in his place. Most likely, he will not expect you to be prepared with some weapon, so he will be overwhelmed by the pain.

Chapter 2 - Useful Defensive Tips and Tricks

If you are interested in being effective in your efforts, you need to be smart about what you are going to do. The following are some of the simplest, but valuable strategies you can take with you to any battle:

- *Choose the nearest target possible.* The element of surprise is your most important weapon. You can only surprise an attacker if you are quick with your action. For instance, why should you punch a person on the face, if your mere aim will bring an alarm so that your attacker could avoid it or hit your first? Instead of blowing a punch to the face, you can kick a person on the knee and immediately disarm him.

- *Make some noise.* When an attacker has come to conquer you, make some noise. Do not hesitate to yell at the top of your lungs, even if you think there is no one there because you do not know who could be near enough to hear you. The sound you make will distract your attacker and will bring him unease. Chances are he will become nervous and flee for his own safety.

- *Know the strength of your hand.* If you are going to strike anyone with your hand, use the outer edge of your hand, with a knife-hand position, knuckle-blow or palm strike.

- *Find a weapon in everyday objects.* Since attacks can come anytime and anywhere, it is most likely that you will not be prepared with a weapon. The absence of a "true" weapon does not automatically translate to defeat. Survey your surroundings and find weapons in things like a pen, key or hairspray. Be imaginative with the use of things around you and use it well to your advantage.

- *Refuse to be controlled.* Your attacker will want to overpower you, so show him that you are unwilling to succumb to his power by going berserk. If you cannot effectively defend yourself, keep the movement solid and constant. Start hitting, kicking, punching and throwing. Keep moving and do not allow yourself to be controlled—just give him a hard time.

- *Know your limit.* You have to know which fights could be fought. If your attacker has a weapon and you know in your heart that you are no match for it, then yield. If the attacker is trying to mug you, give your wallet. A knife in your chest or a bullet in your head is not going to be worth it.

- *Your strongest knuckles.* It is quite easy to throw the wrong punch. As a matter of fact, the wrong punch will have you hurt yourself more than your attacker. If you are going to strike with your closed fists, remember to use your biggest knuckles. Also, throw your punch along with your entire body for the extra force.

- *Your goal is not to win.* Since this is not a competition, but a fight for life and safety, do not be afraid to run away as soon as there is an opportunity. Your main goal is to stay safe and to avoid the legal ramifications of hurting someone else necessarily.

- *Use your shins to kick.* Many people make the mistake of aiming with the foot or knee during a kick. If you want to bring more damage, you need to aim with your shin.

- *Do not try to be a movie star.* Even if it looks good on Jackie Chan, do not expect that his movie moves will work well in real life situations. Do not try to be fancy with your moves. Your goal is to stay safe and to hit your attacker, do not make things complicated, by trying to be some kind of amazing fighter—when the truth is that you are not.

- *Stay calm.* Even if the situation is completely stressful, try to get on top of things and stay calm. You will best function when you can think straight and are not immediately overcome by hearing. Try to remember everything you've learned and applied it accordingly.

- *Hit him first.* Your best chance is always to get your attacker by surprise so be in control of the situation and hit him first. Taking note of the body's weakest points, see which body part is most exposed and hit it. You do this so that you can disable him and make your next move. This next move may be to flee or to fight, some more.

- *Keep your hands up.* Every boxing trainer will tell you this, "Keep your hands up." This stance will keep you alert so that you can hit at every opportunity and at the same time, block blows that come your way.

- *Grappling and locks do not have room in real life.* Although many self-defense training classes will involve strategies on how to lock and grapple, you cannot rely on these moves to actually defeat your attacker. In movies, these things magically save the day, but this may not work in real life, so reserve your energy for defensive techniques that bring forth more damage.

- *Understand that attackers are ready to fight back.* In class, most drills end after you have succeeded with a specific move. In real life, an attacker will not care who you are. He will fight back, and he will inflict pain in the best way he can. You have to be prepared for attackers who will stop at nothing until he completely defeats you. Your best defense here is to flee and run as fast as you ca towards safety.

- *Maintain a defensive posture.* Always be on the defensive. It is good if you can throw a damaging offensive attack, but always be on guard. Apart from keeping your hands up, to guard your face; you have to keep a steady stance and keep your feet planted on the floor. Carefully and effectively assess your attacker and while you are doing all these, position yourself to run away. Your goal is to protect yourself and to maintain your safety, at all times. There shouldn't be anything in your mind but that.

- *Try not to be obvious.* The biggest mistake you can make when in confronted by an attacker is to let him know what defensive attack you are going to launch. Do not look at his left shoulder, if you plan to attack it. Similarly, do not make it obvious that you are about to hit his knee. Look straight at your attacker so that he does not know what your next move will be. Your best chance is always the element of surprise.

- *Speak a different language.* This kind of trickery may or may not work, but it is worth trying. You are relying on heightening the frustration levels of your attacker, so when he engages you, try to speak in a different language so that he cannot understand you. If it does not completely throw him off, you can at least buy some valuable time.

- *Press all keys in the elevator.* If you are in an elevator and you are suspecting that the other person in the elevator with you is a potential attacker, press all the keys. This will mean that the elevator will stop on all floors and he will be prevented to make a move. As soon as you see a floor with people, race out of the small space and go out in the open.

- *Do not stand still.* If you are confronted in the street, and your attacker is approximating you, the worst thing you can do is to stand still. It will be easier to make you a target if you do so. Move about, and if you have running skills, run as fast as you can. Survey the area quickly and find a nice escape route.

Self Defense Drills

Self-defense and protecting yourself ought to be a lifestyle. Danger is around us, and you need to make a good habit of always keeping yourself protected. The following drills are exercises that you can carry out with friends and family. Some of these drills are applied in the different classes. Use these in your training.

1. Continuous Self Defense Exercise

    This is a very basic drill, and you can do this on your own. Using every strategy you have learned from this book or in class, you just have to perform all the self-defense moves one after the other. You do not need an opponent. This drill is about mastery.

2. Self-Defense Line

    This is drill is nice to do with a few people. You have to form a straight line and one after the other; you have to defend yourself as your instructor comes to attack you. Using everything you have learned, you have to match his attack with an appropriate move. Everyone gets his turn. After performing the move, he goes to the end of the line, and the next one goes.

3. The Round Robin Self-Defense Drill

This is a very fun and interactive self-defense drill because it gives you a chance to train with everyone in the group. Everyone forms a circle with the instructor or leader in the middle. The person in the middle makes his round to everyone, and once he completes the cycle, a new person is taking place in the middle. This continues until everyone gets the chance to be in the middle. This is a nice and fast-paced drill, and it allows you to pair up with different people.

4. Spontaneous Drill Circle

This kind of drill tests is a good way to practice your alertness to fend for yourself and counter attack. A circle is formed by a single person standing in the middle, waiting for an attack to come from any direction. One by one, people from the circle will come forward to attack. This can follow a time limit. The person in the middle will have to continuously defend himself until the time lapses.

5. Hands On the Side Defense

In a real life situation, you will not know where danger is going to come so you will not be prepared. As there is really no perfect way to simulate this, the only thing you can do is start with your hands on the side. Standing in the center of the room, with your hands on the side, you let attacks come from different directions and defend you accordingly. The element of surprise will be more, compared to when you are already geared for a block and standing in a stable stance.

6. Defending Against Two Attackers

Sometimes you will be faced with two different attackers, and you have to be prepared for this situation. This drill will have you positioned in the middle, in front of two attackers standing on either side. This drill assumes that your attackers will grab onto your shoulder. As soon as the hands take place on your shoulder, you perform this sequence on both attackers:

    a. Two-handed block
    b. Two-handed reverse shuto to neck
    c. Two-handed shuto to throat
    d. Two-handed back fist to nose
    e. Two-handed hammer fist to groin
    f. Right palm to the nose of the person on the left
    g. Right elbow to the face of the person on the left
    h. Left spinning back fist landing on the nose of the person on the right
    i. Right hook punch to the nose of the person on the right

    j. Right side kick to the knee of the person on the right
    k. Left side kick to the knee of the person on the left

7. Defending The Push

Attackers always enter with a push. They push because it stuns and disables a victim, who often falls on the floor. If your attacker approaches you this way, you have to be prepared to counteract the move. The following are some drills you can practice against the push:

    a. The Inside Block

- Start with a two-handed shuto chop on the attacker's shoulder
- Right-hand shuto chop to neck
- Left hand shuto chop to groin

    b. The Outside and Down Block

- Knee kick or pelvic groin kick
- Right-hand strike chin with upward elbow move
- Right-hand strike nose with down palm heal move

c. One Hand Up and One Hand Down
   - Right palm straight and down to nose
   - Left palm to lower chin with a heel strike
   - Right palm with fingers down to groin
   - Left palm to face with heel strike
   - Right elbow straight to jaw

8. The Square Target Drill

This is a nice drill to do with another person. You can take turns being the attacker and defender. The attacker should have his hands padded, but the defender will have empty hands. This will be performed like a rhythmic dance.

   a. Attacker launches a right punch; Defender launches a left-handed slap down
   b. Attacker launches a left hook; Defender launches a right-handed inside block
   c. Attacker launches a right punch; Defender launches a left-handed slap down
   d. Attacker holds the target out; Defender launches the right elbow on the attacker
   e. Attacker holds the target out; Defender launches the left elbow on the attacker

9. The Push and Pull Drill

This is another two-person drill. These set of drills will help prepare you for attackers whose initial move on you is either push or pull.

   a. Against the Push
      - Attacker pushes you on the left shoulder, and you do not resist
      - Turn in the direction of the push and block it the attacker's hand using your left hand
      - Launch a right hook on the face
      - Hit the right elbow
      - Strike the groin with the left hand or knee

   b. Against the Pull
      - Attacker pulls your left shoulder, and you do not resist
      - Block and grab the left arm
      - Hit the right elbow
      - Hit the right knew
      - Launch a forward push to send them away

10. Walking Along Enemy Lines

This is a brilliant group drill. You should draw two lines to form a center aisle. A person walks down the line, and three people will launch an attack from either side.

The person does not know where the attack is going to come from and he launches three defensive moves accordingly.

Everyone in the team takes his turn to walk down the aisle until everyone gets to perform.

11. Tennis Ball / Bean Bag Toss Drill

Sometimes the best drills are those that actually provide you with a good foundation, and this is a good example. Attackers come from any direction, and this exercise is meant to increase the accuracy of your peripheral vision. It is also designed to improve your reaction time and your hand/eye coordination.

Start the drill with the bean bad. Face a wall and assign a point to focus on. Look straight into that space and with your left hand, toss the bean bag to the right hand at eye level, and let the right hand catch it with the palm up. Do not look at the bag or at your hands. Keep looking straight. Keeping throwing the bean bag from hand to hand and when you have mastered this, throw the bag a little higher until you progress to a point where you cannot even see the bean bag anymore.

As soon as you have mastered the bag, you may progress to the tennis ball. This will be a little trickier because it is going to be harder to grip. Follow the same progressive drill you performed with the bean bag.

12. Practicing Footwork Drills

Self-defense is also about speed, and when you are quick on your toes, you can effectively defend yourself from harm. This set of footwork drills will be good for your timing, speed, and reflexes.

Stand with your feet at shoulder-width apart, with your strong foot a step forward from the other. The move is quite simple. You move left and right. To move left, you put your weight on the right foot and push with your left foot and then let your right foot slide to follow the movement. To move right, you put your weight on the left foot and push with your right foot and let your left foot slide to follow the movement. You can do this in front of the television or with music playing.

If you are doing this in front of the television, you move right and left, changing directions every time scenes change in a show. If you are doing this with music, you move right and left, changing directions every time a new stanza is begun.

A good upgrade to this move is to add a forward and backward to the movement. Raise the level once you have mastered the right and left movements.

Handling Weapons

This section of your self-defense training focuses on the more organized armed attack. Most people are not comfortable owning weapons, but if that is not an issue with you, then understand that you are safer with a weapon. Especially if you learn the proper handling of your weapon of choice, you can maximize your advantage against any kind of attacker.

Gun Drills

1. Get Back and Fire

    Regardless if you are armed with a gun and feeling confident, never engage to meet an attacker. Instead, engage the attacker while moving back and shouting "Get back." The words are spoken because, in the courtroom, these statements may be used to justify any outcome. With your hand pointed straight at your attacker, who is also armed, you fire two shots on the center mass (pelvic girdle or head). You should keep firing until you land two solid hits. Make sure to shout 'Get back", so you will get used to it.

    Keep working on this drill until you are able to land two solid shots with precision, even when you are moving backward.

2. The First Shot Drill

In a gun fight, always remember that it is crucial who lands the first shot because if you successfully land a shot on your attacker, you immediately increase your chance of escaping to safety.

With your gun in the holster and your hands raised up, as if in surrender, position yourself 10 yards away from the target and at the sound of the buzzer, pull your gun from the holster, ready it from safety, aim and then fire. A good gun handler can achieve a good center hit in 1.5 seconds that is great speed. Keep running this drill until you are more efficient and fluid with your move.

3. Straight to the Head to End It

In some situations, you have already engaged your attacker and have delivered body shots, but he is still advancing on you. A good way to finally put the man down is to hit a solid shot to the head. This is also known as the Mozambique Drill or the Failure Drill and was developed by Mike Rousseau. When the attacker wasn't downed with two rounds of shots on the body, he aimed at the head to finally take him down.

For this drill, you need to set a silhouette to obscure the attacker and position yourself about 21 feet away. At the start of the drill, you will need to fire two shots to the center mass and check if the attacker is still coming forward to your direction. Finally, take that shot to the head. You can increase the difficulty of the drill by adding barriers and other covers so you can practice moving around.

4. Shooting Until the Threat Is Eliminated

This was designed by Kyle Lamb and is also known as the 1-5 Drill, and it teaches you to forget the lazy double tap that is often unreliable. Most drill train you to shoot a double tap and to flee, but then you will find that the attacker has not been downed, so you have to engage him again. This will only put you more danger. This drill makes sure that the target is down and eliminated.

You arrange three targets about five yards away from you and about target away from each other. When the buzzer sounds, you shoot land shots this way: 1 one the left, 2 on the center, 3 on the right, 4 on the center and finally 5 on the left target. In total, you will fire 15 shots, and you should endeavor to finish this drill in less than 3.5 seconds. Keep running this until you are more precise, even with speed.

5. Away from the X

As with any gun situation, your goal is to escape your attacker. This drill practices your efficiency to escape from the area of the fight, so you move backward or in a diagonal direction while maintaining gun engagement with your attacker.

Looking straight towards your target, X, you move away and land as many shots as you can. You can upgrade the level of this drill by adding obstacles and areas for cover. In real life, obstacles will be present, and you need to know how to maneuver yourself through these different objects while firing a gun.

6. The Physical Pressure Drill

In a practice setup, you may feel a little nervous and pressure, but it will in no way simulate the rising tension that you experience in the real setting. In a real encounter with an attacker, your heart will raise, and you will even find it hard to breathe and move.

To simulate this situation, this drill will involve getting your heart pumping, by including push-ups, side-straddle hops, sit-ups, and sprints, while you complete the course. The course will be lengthy and will involve a lot of running—and it will involve stopping for some exercise, to get your heart going. The physical strain will mimic a real life stress in gunfight situations and prepare you for the real thing.

7. The Triple Mozambique

This drill will practice your accuracy and speed. In a threatening situation, you will not have all the time in the world, so this drill is going to be of true value. It is not difficult, but it is just about landing the shots and doing so in the fastest way possible. An experienced shooter can do this drill in 3-5 seconds.

Arrange three targets at 15 yards and at the buzzer, double tap the targets at the center and then land one on the head. If a bullet lands outside the A-zone add 2 seconds to the time. If a shot completely misses, add 5 seconds per shot. Keep running this drill until you develop accuracy and speed.

8. The Dummy Round Drill

You should recognize that in real life situations, anything can happen. You cannot expect that things will always go as you have learned it in classes. The truth is that most of than not, things will not go according to plan, and this drill should prepare for you for such.

If you can employ someone to fill magazine rounds for you, tell this person to fill a round with dummies. You will have good magazine rounds and one that is absolutely empty.

You run the drill by going through an obstacle course that you prepared, engaging the target with two taps, at each time. When you load the magazine with the dummies, you will not be able to fire so you will be caught off guard. With much speed, you have to reload with the proper magazine and proceed with the drill. This will help improve your composure, which will be a good asset in a real-life situation.

9. Your Reaction Time

This is a very creative "action vs. reaction" drill. It is nothing fancy, but it shows you the reality that you may not realize about firing a gun and more specifically, your advantage when firing the gun.

This drill is simple. You have to stand with the gun in your holster and a second person is standing behind you. At the sound of the buzzer the person runs, while your try to take a shot at the target. The other person stops running as soon as the gun fires. This will show you the reality of your speed and the significance that time can make for your safety.

Fighting with the Knife

There are many weapons that you will encounter in the real world, which may be used against you, or you can use for your defense. A knife is going to be one of them. Contrary to what many people think about the knife, however, it is not always a reliable weapon (unlike a firearm). It has its advantages—and many attackers use it, but here is a closer look at knife-fighting that you may find quite valuable.

1. Drawing the knife out. This is actually true in most fights where weapons are involved. In the classroom, you will be learning about drawing weapons out, at the sign of danger and you have probably mastered taking your gun or knife out, but when the pressure is real—the whole picture changes. Most of the time, before you even remember that you have a knife, you have already been attacked. What is more valuable, therefore, is protecting yourself against knife attacks.

2. There won't be a knife fight. This is not a movie where the magnificent knife handling skills will be jaw dropping. When an attacker crosses your path, he will come for the "kill" there is no need for your fancy knife moves because he will go straight to where he can do the most damage.

3. The knife is not an extension of your hand. Many teachers will try to encourage you to learn knife skills so that your movements with unarmed combat will be enhanced. What they are suggesting is that you will be able to translate all the unarmed principles you have learned, and perform them with a knife. What is true is that the knife is an extension of your will to fight. It is placed in your hand so that it may boost your confidence, but it does not necessarily raise your fighting ability. All weapons function the same way.

4. The value of knife drills. One thing should be clear. In the classroom, when you learn knife drills, you are learning principles and ideas, and they will be the framework of your skill. What you learn in the classroom does not automatically translate to a battlefield. Knife use deal so much about angles, range, position—and none of these will be ideal in real life.

5. Cutting yourself. When you are holding a weapon, such as a knife, expect that in the struggle, you can also cut yourself. Knives are very hard to handle, even for so-called experts, and when you incapacitate yourself with your own weapon, then that will bring forth an unfortunate turn of events.

Chapter 3 - Mental Defense

Contrary to what most people believe the most effective defensive countermeasure is one that is not purely physical. Self-defense involves a great deal of mental mindset, so the training usually involves the display of mental toughness and tenacity.

Every fighter is encouraged to develop a warrior mindset that allows one to leave the training ground, and realize that the world is one big fighting ring. Your physical skill in the classroom may be calculated to perfection, but you should realize that is not what happens in real life.

Ultimately, it is your mental capacity that sees you through the whole obstacle. It is a self-preserving skill that pushes you to move forward, even when your body is ready to quit.

Developing the Correct Mindset

Believe it our not, you could be properly trained and equipped in the classroom, but if you are not ready for the battle, all your knowledge will be good for nothing. Self-defense is two-fold, and for your efforts to be truly successful, you need to develop the right mindset to give true power to your punch.

When your body and mind is ready, your defense is going to be solid enough to defeat even the most powerful attacker.

What do you need to be in the right condition?

- Visualize dangers in your mind. When you have thought of it enough, it will feel as though you have been through it already. In the gym or classroom, it is not easy to recreate a true situation, even if a simulation is created. The truth is that nothing will truly represent the real thing, but you have to imagine it in your head as if it is truly happening. Think of different situations and imagine yourself going through them. How will you deal with it? Make a habit of imagining different scenarios. Sometimes watching action films and thrillers help open your mind to these situations. You need to try to bring yourself to the situation so you can pretend to deal with it.

- Memorize your first line of defense. Endeavor to carve in your mind the "moves" you will carry out as soon as the danger arises. It may never be easy to apply these things in a real crisis, but this kind of mind condition sets up the mind so that it is always ready when to react with precision. The worst thing that could happen is for you to have a booklet worth of self-defensive strategies but none that you can think of in the first split second. When it is carved in your mind, it will become as natural as taking air in to breathe. It will be purposeful and exact.

- Understand your motivation to stay alive. It is not to quit and let the chips fall as they should. It is not letting things happen because you have no choice. You may not have control over when dangers happen and how they will unfold, but you should make a decision to fight for your safety and to stay alive. That should be clear in your heart and in your mind. Your want for safety should be clear enough so that it is enough motivation to throw that definitive punch. Your want for safety should be clear enough so that it is enough motivation to break free and run away. You need to highlight your motivation because it is not going to be easy. When your attacker has overcome you and has his grip on your neck, it will be easier to succumb to his power, but it doesn't mean that you should.

- Do not give yourself too many responses. You might think that increasing your physical self-defense portfolio will guarantee success, but it won't. It will never be about how many moves you know, that saves, you. It will not be about memorizing as many strategies that matter because the overload will actually confuse you. Find your strengths and concentrate on the mastering these moves, so that you may make yourself more effective.

Understanding the Mind of the Attacker

Your attacker could be anybody. It does not have to be the typical image of a villain. It does not have to be a man. It does not have to be someone who is wrapped in tattoos or facial hair. An attacker could be anyone— even someone you least expect it to be, but a few things will be true: your attacker picked you because they know they can defeat you.

You have to understand their motivations for choosing you as their victim because if you do, then you will have a better chance of winning. Why did you attacker choose you?

- They are confident about their size. A person who is bigger (in height and size) will feel more powerful. Height is might, they say, that is why Goliath laughed at David when he challenged him to a fight. But of course, we know who won that battle.

- They are confident about their strength. Apart from the strength that is dictated by size, some people are just strong, and they know it. If you look weak, then you will become an easy victim. Attackers will choose you, for the mere reason that they find you easy to overcome and dominate.

- They are skilled in the art of fighting. There are true strength and confidence that is developed in a person when he has trained in the art of fighting. Someone who has mastered any kind of martial art will feel confidence about his capacity to defeat you.

- They are armed with a weapon. Weapons give anyone, false strength. When your attacker is armed with a weapon, and you are not, he will definitely see this as an advantage. An attacker may choose you for the reason that he is armed and you are not. Finding an opponent always means finding someone whom you can defeat and the clear advantage that the weapon provides, determines your fate.

- They can outnumber you. If an attacker is with someone else and you are alone, he will be confident about the number and take advantage of it. A companion almost automatically improves an attacker's chance of defeating a victim because companions can add force to the attack.

- You are distracted. You may be distracted in so many ways. Maybe you are engaged in a call, busy working with something, and so forth. If your full attention is absent in the situation, it will be easy to attack you by surprise. You wouldn't know what hit you because you are unprepared and unexpecting.

- You are injured. Injury is always seen as a weakness. If you are limping, missing a limb or in an obvious physical disadvantage, an attacker may take advantage of his chance to dominate you.

Sometimes, it has nothing to do about you, but when a person is under the influence of alcohol or drugs, he may not be in the right mind to control his emotions. Sometimes an attacker has no character for violence, but he will be capable of inflicting pain because of altered consciousness. What is most worrying about these people is that they often feel as though they are equipped with super powers, while under the influence, so they know no bounds. Your best protection against these people is to stay away from them. If you smell danger, try your best to flee at once.

Threat Assessment

A good part of mental self-defense involves effective threat assessment. This is a violence prevention strategy that helps a person to:

a. identify the threat even before intention is actually signified
b. determine how serious the threat is
c. be able to carry out an instantaneous defensive act to counter the threat

Everyone studying self-defense needs to understand the importance of threat assessment because the smartest self-defensive strategy is to avoid danger. You can only do this when you are full aware of what is going on around you so that you can escape.

Instinct is the most reliable weapon in threat assessment. This is often based on compounded life stories from personal experience and the experience of others. When you watch the news and read newspapers, you come to know the reality of danger, even from afar. If you want to develop your ability to detect danger, a thorough analysis of various situations can open your mind. This will help you identify patterns, so that you may be more aware of potential dangers.

Part 1: Analyzing Situational Components

> Study different situations and be familiar with frequency and pattern. Study the details closely, and hopefully, it will become ingrained in you, so recognizing threats will become automatic.
>
> - Location: Where did the incident take place?
>
>   Knowledge of location helps you identify "bad areas" or vulnerable situations that will most likely be unsafe. The house is usually a safe

sanctuary, but many women get assaulted in their own homes if they are alone. Dark alleys, crowded places, and cars are also examples of threat areas. If these areas are common "scenes of crimes," it is best that you stay away.

- Relationship: Who is the attacker? Is he/she related to the victim?

  Most of the time, the attacker is a stranger, and the victim is picked at random, based on convenience and a high chance of success. It is least likely for danger to come from a familiar face, but it is not exactly uncommon. Many have faced danger in the hands of family and so-called friends. Women are often attacked by people they know. To understand this more, you have to look into the next component.

- Motive: Why did the attacker assault the victim?

  Motive, however irrational and distorted, gives meaning to the assault. Any attacker will have a reason that ultimately fuels his act, and it could be pre-meditated or completely a spur-of-the-moment kind of thing.

Understanding motives will allow you to delve deeper into the likelihood of danger to come your way. If you have crossed someone or have been in the middle of something big with some controversial personalities, you should be on guard.

- Third parties: Is the victim with someone else, during the attack?

Most attacks happen when a victim is alone and most vulnerable. It doesn't matter, however, if there are third parties present in the scene because threats can take place anytime and anywhere. In other words, you should not automatically feel safe, just because you are with someone. Some companions flee at danger or scream, but will not offer physical assistance. Some companions even become a liability.

- State of mind: What state of mind was the victim in? Was he/she ready or was he/she distracted?

It is the state of mind of the victim that ultimately defines the course and outcome of the attack. When a victim is in a state of panic, he/she is easier to overcome. Panic often clouds a person's judgment, so he is unable to make quick decisions that ultimately save his life

Some self-defense courses are designed to mimic these conditions closely so that you can take yourself into the situation and best prepare for it. Of all the components, a realistic state of mind is the hardest to duplicate, but it can be considered.

Chapter 4 - The Scope and Limitations of Physical and Mental Self-Defense

It has been reiterated in this book that self-defense is two-fold. Defending yourself is not only achieved through physical training because what is true is that focussing on the physicality of self-preservation has its limitations:

- Many self-defense classes are patterned from disciplines in various traditional martial arts and combat sports. The technicality may seem impressive and powerful, but many of these things are very hard to apply in real life. In this case, it won't matter how many classes you enroll yourself in, if you cannot bring your training to practical use, it will all be for nothing.

- Proficiency is never guaranteed for every student. Some people are just not physically built to perform, and it has nothing to do with the kind of discipline, the intensity of training, or the capacity of the instructor to impart knowledge. Some people are not built for the physicality of these things, so proficiency and effectiveness in this sense may never be guaranteed.

- It is hard to bring reality to the training ground. Earlier situational components were looked into, and these details are taken into account so that they may be simulated in training. Unfortunately, no amount of "fabrication" can actually mimic a real life threat, so your level of expertise in the classroom setup may never translate to actual events.

- Age and physical limitations factor into the success. While proficiency is not guaranteed, your obvious physical limitations will also be a problem. Sometimes it does not matter how well you perform, your limitations will not change anything, especially if your attacker is younger, bigger, stronger, and more agile.

- Attackers will always be at an advantage. You have to understand this as truth because when an attacker pushes for assault, he will make sure he is at an advantage. He will pick the situational components that will ensure victory. Nothing will be in your favor—at least in his standpoint that's certain. This is why there is hardly no guarantee when you rely put all your focus on this aspect of self-defense. Chances are, your attacker is more prepared, and you will not stand a chance.

Threat assessment is effective when you are able to defend yourself, even before, the actual need arises.

Understand that the few moments before the attack is launched is very crucial and when you are able to identify indicators, your chances of survival are increased. Here are some of the things you need to look for:

- Sending signals. If you notice two or more people sending non-verbal messages and signals to each other, you have to be wary. These signals may be their cue to launch the attack so open your eyes for these things. If you are able to intercept any kind of signal, your entire story can chance.

- Correlation of movement. More than the signals, a more definitive sign of threat would be a movement that relates to your own movements. When you notice that your suspected attacker(s) seems to be going where you're going—stopping and turning when you do, keep your guard up.

- Cornering. As you become more attainable, you will notice that your attacker(s) is working on moving you to a place where trapping you is going to be easier. This is most likely a corner or an enclosed area where escape is not possible.

- Intent focus and attention. Ready to pounce and determined not to let you go, it will feel as though you are put under a spotlight because all the attention will be concentrated on you.

He will not allow for you to escape, so a tight watch will be put on you.

- Concealment. If the attacker is carrying a weapon, you will notice that they will become more obvious about what they are trying to conceal. He may have a hand inside the coat, or he may be reaching into a pocket. The hands will be geared for the next move, and that pulls out a weapon and launch the attack.

- Movement of hands. If the hands are visible, where is it? An attacker who is ready to make a move will be positioning himself at an advantage. Watch the hands, if it is not yet concealed because as soon as it goes in to grab something, things will start to unfold.

- Looking over the shoulder. An attacker may be at an advantage, but he is a criminal (in the making) nonetheless. He will definitely feel afraid of getting caught so he will be looking over his shoulders, to make sure that no one is onto him. The worst thing to happen to an attacker is to be found out before the attack is even launched, so he will definitely be afraid of his own shadow.

These signs will be visible just before the assault actually takes place. It may or may not be too late for you to flee, but recognizing these threats will signify true danger, and you need to be aware of it.

Other Forms of Self Defense

The effectiveness of one's self-defense strategy combines the physical and mental capacity of the individual to rise above the situation. As prevention of harm is always better, understand that there is also wisdom in the following:

Personal Alarms

Personal alarms come in different forms. But it is basically a passive defensive mechanism that one can utilize in order to signify danger. A child who is unable to physically and mentally defend himself may be fitted with a personal alarm, and he can trigger it to give off a loud sound that calls the public's attention.

These personal alarms also work as good locators. A person may not be in danger of an attack but is in trouble by some other means.

Avoidance

Avoidance is being aware of the danger and getting away from the potential harm and injury. It recognizes the threat, even before it manifests so that you can prevent any negative outcome. In movies, you see Bruce Lee colliding with and victoriously surviving a battalion of warriors, but your life is not a movie.

Understand that ambush attacks always put the defender at a disadvantage. If you think you will be compromised, do not try to be a hero. Find a way to avoid danger and recognize any opportunity to escape so you can take it.

The following are some effective safety measures that will help you avoid danger:

- Always be aware of your surroundings. All be suspicious and never allow yourself to be completely overcome by the situation. If the area is a potentially dangerous area, you should be more cautious. Nevertheless, always be alert and mindful of threat signals. This is most true if you are approaching your car. In movies, this is a very predictable danger scene.

- Try not to be alone. Especially if you are going to be in a threatening area, you need to be with someone. If it is unavoidable, make sure to stay in well-lit areas. Avoid dark corners where it is going to be easier for you to be attacked.

- Do not be predictable. Try to avoid patterns are routines so that people cannot plan their attack based on your unbreakable routine. Some attackers prey on people whom they can study closely because the predictability is a big giveaway.

De-escalation

The tongue is a powerful weapon, especially if you have a good command of words. Conflict management is the skill of a person to take a potentially harmful situation to a less harmful one. When tensions are high, and the raging tempers are about to explode, one can handle the uproar and bring it down and in control. The simple calling of a "time out" effectively dissipates the rising anger coming from all directions. De-escalation involves a level of empathic capability to touch an attacker's emotion and soothe it.

Walk With Confidence

It may not seem much but understand that when people find their victims, they eye the crowd for someone they can dominate. A predator always goes for someone that they can overcome, so a good way to avoid being under threat is to act confident. If you cannot exude genuine confidence, then you should at least pretend to be strong. And hopefully, the level of pretention you display is enough to convince attackers against approaching you.

Walking with confidence sends out a positive image. To do this, you have to wear your head talk and keep your shoulders up. You should send an air of superiority even if you are shattering inside.

Pre-Incident Indicators (PINS)

PINS or Pre-Incident Indicators was discussed in Gavin Becker's books called "The Gift of Fear." A good defense is always one that helps you avoid danger. It has been discussed several times in this book, and it will be discussed again. When you find yourself in contact with a stranger, you have to be wary of the following behavior so that you can protect yourself from any potential danger.

The following are some of the suspicious behavior you need to take note of:

- Refusing your "NO." If a stranger offers to do something for you and you say "NO" he should politely accept it. If he refuses your "NO" and insists on still helping you, against your will, chances are these is a hidden agenda.

- Being too charming. Kindness is a good trait, but when someone is too good to be true, it becomes frightening. Some people use kindness as a way to manipulate people. They use kindness to disarm you, and when you have your guard down, they will attack.

- Showing sympathy for your predicament. A good way to engage a target is to sympathize with the person's predicament. Some strangers will try to find something in common with you so they can capture your attention. They will sympathize with your emotion, with hopes that you open up to them.

- Offering too many details. When a person is lying, he will overcompensate with details, in an effort to sound more credible. If the story sounds too elaborate and perfectly sewn together, be suspicious. If a person is trying to justify his presence with a million reasons, it feels rather unnecessary.

- Giving unsolicited help with the expectation of favors. Sometimes a person who has successfully broken into you will take it a step further and entrap you because he has helped you. "That was a tiring four flights of stairs. Let me just breathe for a second." And because you feel bad, you will offer a glass of water or a moment to sit down. This is a stranger that you have just given permission to enter into your house. It wasn't your intention, in the first place, but it all just happened too fast.

- Typecasting. Some people will use an insult in order to break you down. He will insult your kindness or understanding, so you will be forced to give in to his conditions, just to defend yourself. It is very easy to get trapped into a situation like this. An attacker has the capacity to play with your emotion and ego—if you allow him, he will use it against you.

This situation with another person can happen out of the ordinary, and it may seem rather harmless, but this kind of contact can often lead to disastrous events. If you find yourself in these situations, find a way to get yourself out of it. These people may or may not have bad intentions with you—are you really going to wait for something bad to happen?

Screaming

Screaming is an armless weapon, and on the subject of self-defense, people will have varying thoughts about shouting at the top their lungs. Some people regard it as a useless move because it wastes time; but others will encourage the creation of noise, to alert people nearby, to come to your attention and rescue.

The power and value of screaming are undetermined until it is performed. But you have to make time to do it because it has the capacity to save your life. Some attackers will be threatened with the scream and run away, for fear of getting compromised. Some attackers will detest your action and harm you for doing it. The truth is that it can go both ways and you have to prepare yourself for what might happen.

You scream, at the top of your lungs, because in a tight situation, it may be your only option.

Self Defense Classes

It does not matter if you are a man or a woman, you have the right to defend yourself against people who want to bring harm to you. If you are not equipped to protect yourself, you can enroll yourself in classes. There are various places that offer self-defense training, and the courses are designed according to the capacity and need of the individual.

If you are intent on enrolling in such classes, you have to consider the following details:

- Observe the class first. Before enrolling in a class, you can spend some time to observe the class and get a feel of it. Observe the teachers and the students. Is this the kind of learning environment that you wish to become a part of? Do you like the feel of the class? You do not have to enroll in a program without knowing what you are getting yourself into.

- It should be endorsed by law enforcement agents and security professionals. If you want to be sure about the credibility of the class you are taking, it is smart to look for an endorsement from self-defense experts. There are several classes you can take and so many people claiming to know what they're doing. Only trust one with the credible endorsement so you can rest assured that you are in good hands.

- It should offer a variety of techniques. There are countless disciplines applied in self-defense, and while some have roots from traditional martial arts, others are more modern and practical in approach. Choose a school that offers a great variety of things so that you can find the best discipline for your own use.

- You should trust your instructor. As you are relying on one or a few people to instill in you the right skills that eventually shall save your life, you need to choose a school that is made up of people whom you can trust. However indirectly, you are choosing this person to protect you and save you from harm. This person should genuinely care for your safety and well-being so he will equip you with whatever is effective and necessary. He will sure to teach you all that you need and will not cut corners because he values your life, just as you do.

- It should approach self-defense holistically. As already learned, self-defense involves both the physical and mental discipline. An effective class is one that not just focuses on one aspect, but rather conquers it as a whole. You need to be physically and mentally ready for the battle ahead. You can only be prepared if your school and teachers, share the same goal.

- You should be having fun. Self-defense is not exactly something you take lightly, but for you to achieve mastery of the said art, you need to gain the right passion for it. Many of the moves will sound too technical if you are looking at it as a task; but if you embrace the whole idea as something enjoyable, things will definitely change. As a matter of fact, the moment you begin to enjoy the classes, you will notice that moves become easier to achieve. Take learning as an adventure and an interesting challenge. Do not let the technicalities intimidate you because if you let it, how else can you overcome your attacker?

The Legalities of Self Defense

Throughout the book, it has been expressed, right from the start, that in any given situation, you should protect your safety. Your life is your responsibility, and it is universally accepted for one to protect himself from harm. Unfortunately, there are legal boundaries for self-defense, and it is important that you are aware of your limitations, so that you do not end up compromising yourself.

In other words, there is nothing wrong with your desire to protect yourself, but understand that this right is bound by the following principles:

1. Extent of the right to self-protection

   Homicide and robbery have wider limits for self-defense because it is never easy to ascertain as to how far an attacker is willing to go. But in most cases, a threat to violence should exist. Meaning, a victim should use all precautionary measures to prevent the attack.

2. Who serves the right to exercise self-defense

   Ideally, only the person under attack serves the right to exercise self-defense, but in special cases, it may be transferred to close relations such as husband and wives; parent and child; and master and servant.

3. Against whom may a defensive act be exercised

   Self-defense may be performed on the person or persons who launched the attack. This is justifiable whether or not a felony has been attempted.

4. Cause of the defensive act

   This is clear, there should be a threat of danger and a threat to life.

Conclusion

Self-defense is an innate survival practice that may be enhanced and improved, through training. Danger is inevitable, and it can come in all forms, so self-protection is a necessary skill. Anyone may find themselves compromised, even in the safety of their own home. The threat may come from complete strangers, but it may also be launched by a person you know, such as a family member or friend. Nothing is certain anymore, where safety is concerned, so you have to effectively arm yourself with whatever is necessary.

While authorities exist to serve and protect, the crucial moments that actually save your life, rely on your own capacity to prevent harm and counter the act. The value of self-defense is empowerment. In the training field, the enhancement of one's self-defense skills is encouraged because it increases one's chance of surviving an attack.

This book is a guide, and it encourages everyone to seek self-resilience. In the face of danger, anything can happen. But for things to positively go your way, you need to know how to fight for your safety.

Made in the USA
Lexington, KY
02 September 2017